Exotic Arabian Recipes

An Exotically Themed Cookbook of Middle Eastern Dish Ideas!

BY

Stephanie Sharp

Warning - Disclaimer

The purpose of this book is to educate and entertain. The author and does not guarantee that anyone following these techniques, suggestions, tips, ideas, or strategies will become successful. The author shall have neither liability nor responsibility to anyone with respect to any loss or damage caused, or alleged to be caused, directly or indirectly by the information contained in this book.

Thank you so much for purchasing my book! As a reward for your purchase, you can now receive free books sent to you every day. All you have to do is just subscribe to the list by entering your email address in the box below and I will send you a notification every time I have a free promotion running. The books will absolutely be free with no work at all from you!

Who doesn't want free books? No one! There are free and discounted books every day, and an email is sent to you 1-2 days beforehand to remind you so you don't miss out. It's that easy!

Just visit the link or scan QR-code to get started!

https://stephanie-sharp.subscribemenow.com

Table of Contents

Introduction 8

Yogurt with Saffron and Honey 10

Authentic Arabian Vegetable Egg Breakfast Recipe 12

Stuffed Breakfast Paratha 15

Breakfast Shakshouka 18

Arab Banana Breakfast Dish – Masoub 20

Arabian Lunch, Dinner, Appetizer and Side Order Recipes

.... 22

Arabian Meat and Spinach Stew 23

Eggplant Curry el Arabia 26

Arabian Chicken Mugalgal 29

Pickled Beets – Torshi 32

Arabian Kabsa 34

Chicken Haleem 37

Rice Boukhari.. 40

Grilled Arab Kebabs.. 43

Meat and Okra Stew 45

Sheer Khurma.. 48

Arabian Meat Kebab – Kebab el Mirou 50

Ash Reshteh Soup 52

Arabian Tomato and Lamb 55

Leg of Mutton Roast – Raan Roast 57

Arabian Almento Patties 60

Spiced Chicken Shawarma...................................... 63

Noodle & Shish Barak Soup 66

Tahinah Salad.. 68

Arabian Rice with Potato and Lamb 70

Olive Fried Rice 73

Arabian Dessert Recipes 76

Pistachio Cake 77

Sweet Arab Dough Balls 80

Arab Caramel Cardamom Pears 83

Arabian Sweet Cheese Bake 86

Arabian Bread Pudding 88

Conclusion 90

Introduction

What makes Arab cuisine a treat for people who can create and enjoy any type of food they desire?

Arabs use only the finest spices in their dishes. They bring about marvelous aromas of harissa, salona, bukhari, kabsa and other dishes. They are the elements of the Arab world's culinary delights.

The delicious ingredients used in Arabian cooking mean that your first bite may lead to your wanting to try out other dishes from the same taste palette. This is part of the charm of Arab cuisine.

Arabs trace their ancestry to tribes of nomadic herders. Many traditions from the past, including cooking, are maintained today. Traditional foods including the hawayij spice mixture, arikah bread, fatir flatbread and dates are often eaten still today, even though most Arabians live in cities and towns.

Much Arabian food is presented and decorated with special finesse, unknown in many other areas of the world. They give you a wonderfully delightful sensation. Once you try these dishes, you'll be wanting more. Sure, you can find fast food everywhere today, even in the Arab Peninsula, but many people there prefer the more traditional Arabian dishes. You may too, and now you can make some of them in your own kitchen. Turn the page and let's cook!

Yogurt with Saffron and Honey

This is such a light and simple breakfast that is not only delicious, but healthy. It is also eaten during the Sehari time of Ramadan, so it's a versatile dish for almost anytime.

Makes:2 Servings

Cooking + Prep Time: 5 minutes

Ingredients:

- 2 cups of yogurt
- 4 tsp. of honey, pure
- 4 tbsp. of raisins
- 4 tbsp. of flaked coconut
- 1 pinch of saffron

To garnish: almonds

Instructions:

1. Mix all ingredients in your food processor.

2. Pour into glasses. Use almonds to garnish. Serve.

Authentic Arabian Vegetable Egg Breakfast Recipe

This is a seemingly casual gathering of char-grilled vegetables, along with eggs and ricotta. It

makes a wonderful start to your day.

Makes:4 Servings

Cooking + Prep Time: 45 minutes

Ingredients:

- 1 eggplant, large
- 1 tbsp. of oil, olive + 2 tsp. for drizzling
- 2 tbsp. + extra chopped mint leaves
- 7 oz. of ricotta, low-fat, fresh
- 4 eggs, large
- 6 halved tomatoes, Roma, baby
- 2 lengthwise halved cucumbers, Lebanese, small
- 1/2 cup of olives, mixed
- 1 tbsp. of sumac (zaatar)
- 3 & 1/2 oz. of crumbled feta, low-fat
- 2 tbsp. of honey, organic

Instructions:

1. Preheat barbeque grill on med-high.

2. Slice eggplant into eight slices lengthwise. Brush lightly with oil. Grill for two minutes per

side, till they are charred. Set them aside and allow them to cool a bit.

3. Stir mint into ricotta till combined well. Season. When the eggplant has cooled but is still somewhat soft, spread heaping tbsp. of ricotta mixture at one end of first slice. Roll and enclose. Continue with the rest of the eggplants and the ricotta mixture and set them aside.

4. Place eggs in medium pan. Cover them with hot, filtered water. Bring to a boil. Lower heat to med. Simmer for five to six minutes. Remove and place in ice water. Peel and halve the eggs.

5. Divide eggplant rolls, olives, cucumber, tomatoes and eggs on individual plates. Sprinkle eggs using sumac. Crumble feta over plates. Drizzle honey on top. Use extra mint to garnish and drizzle with oil. Serve.

Stuffed Breakfast Paratha

Arabian paratha is lovingly created from fried egg fillings and cooked mince. It sounds hard to make, but it's not, and it tastes especially great if you serve it with pickled vegetables and hummus.

Makes: 4 Servings

Cooking + Prep Time: 1 hour

Ingredients:

For the dough:

- 2 cups of flour, all-purpose
- 1/2 tsp. of salt, sea
- Milk, as needed for kneading

For the filling:

- 10 & 1/2 oz. of mince
- 1 tsp. of garlic-ginger paste
- 1/2 tsp. of salt, sea
- 1/2 tsp. of Chinese salt
- 1/2 tsp. of pepper, black, ground
- 1/2 bunch of coriander, fresh
- 4 chilies, green
- 1 spring onion
- 2 eggs, large
- To fry: clarified butter

For cooking the eggs:

- 1/2 tsp. of pepper, black, ground
- 1/4 tsp. of salt, sea
- 2 tbsp. of oil, olive

Instructions:

1. To prepare the dough, mix the flour and salt and knead with milk to make dough.

2. To prepare the filling, cook mince in pan with salt, water and garlic ginger paste. Cook until mince is tender and water has evaporated.

3. Add green chilies, spring onion, coriander, black pepper and Chinese salt. Combine and turn off burner.

4. Beat eggs separately with sea salt and ground pepper. Heat the oil. Fry the egg mixture in the oil.

5. To prepare the paratha, shape a simple dough ball. Roll the ball out flat and spread the mince filling over it. Spread the egg filling on all sides of dough.

6. Roll and fry in pan with the clarified butter. Serve.

Breakfast Shakshouka

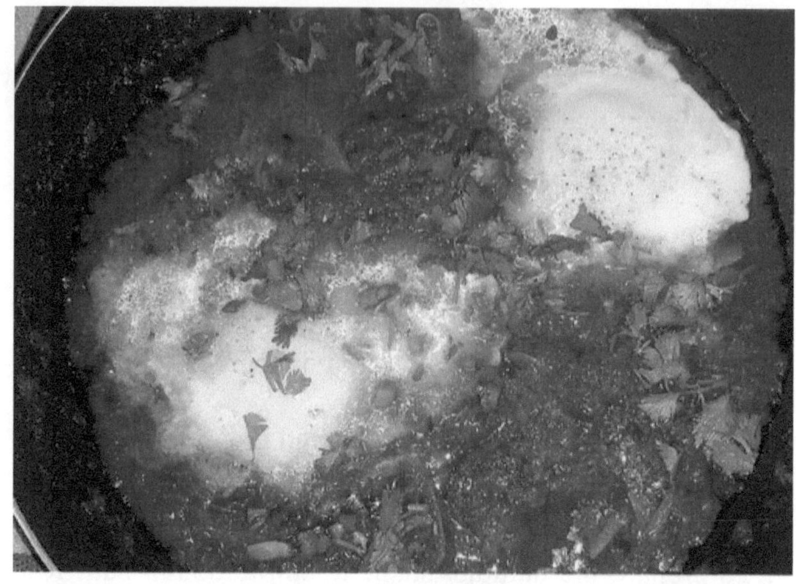

If you've tried shakshouka before, you may wonder how it fits into a breakfast meal. That's why this particular dish, made with fava beans, can redefine breakfast in your household.

Makes: various # servings depending on serving size

Cooking + Prep Time: 1 hour & 10 minutes

Ingredients:

- 1 x 15-16 oz. can of fava beans
- 3 tbsp. of oil, olive
- 3 diced tomatoes, Roma
- 1 medium chopped onion, yellow
- 1 cup of bell peppers, diced
- Salt, sea
- Pepper, ground, black
- 7 eggs, large
- 1/2 tsp. of cumin

Instructions:

1. Sauté the onion in oil on med. heat till it is fragrant.

2. Add the diced tomatoes and stir for several minutes. Add bell peppers. Use salt to season and cook for three to four minutes. Turn burner off.

3. Add beans to baking dish. Top with sautéed veggies.

4. Crack eggs over the top. Sprinkle on sea salt and ground pepper, along with some cumin.

5. Bake for about 1/2 hour, or until done, in 350F oven. Serve.

Arab Banana Breakfast Dish – Masoub

Here is a new and exotic choice for breakfast. Masoub is basically banana bread pudding done in the Arabian way of cooking. It is simple, but so delicious.

Makes: 4 Servings

Cooking + Prep Time: 15 minutes

Ingredients:

- 3 or 4 bananas, very ripe
- 2 or 3 flat breads
- Almonds, sliced
- Raisins, golden
- Whipped cream
- Honey, pure

Optional: mild cheddar shreds

Instructions:

1. In a medium bowl, peel, then mash bananas with fork. Set the bowl aside.

2. Grind flat breads coarsely in food processor. Mix with mashed bananas till combined well. The volume of bread should be roughly the same as that of bananas.

3. Place mixture in serving dish. Smooth the top. Add cheddar, honey, whipped cream, almonds and raisins. Serve.

Arabian Lunch, Dinner, Appetizer and Side Order Recipes

Arabian Meat and Spinach Stew

Tired of trying to get your spouse and children to eat spinach? This meal does the work for you by making it more appealing than ever before. It tastes especially good when served with Arabic bread.

Makes: 5 Servings

Cooking + Prep Time: 2 hours & 10 minutes

Ingredients:

- 2 tbsp. of oil, vegetable
- 2 sliced onions, medium
- 1.10 lb. of cubed lamb
- 1 tsp. of cumin, ground
- 1/2 tsp. of pepper, black, ground
- 2 tbsp. of tomato paste
- 2 chopped tomatoes, medium
- 4 cups of water, filtered
- 2 bouillon cubes, chicken
- 2 fresh spinach bunches
- 1/4 cup of rice, uncooked

Instructions:

1. Chop spinach finely. Wash. Drain and set it aside.

2. Heat vegetable oil in large sized sauce pan. Cook onions till golden - usually five to six minutes.

3. Add the meat. Stir for four to five minutes. Add black pepper and cumin. Stir for a minute.

4. Add bouillon cubes, water, chopped tomatoes and tomato paste. Bring mixture to a boil. Cover pan. Simmer on low heat for 50-60 minutes, till meat becomes tender.

5. Add the rice and spinach. Simmer for 12-15 more minutes, till rice has cooked. Serve hot.

Eggplant Curry el Arabia

Arabic eggplant curry is a wonderful dish of veggies that is a good choice for diabetics, or anyone else in your family. It's an easy dish to make, and people truly love it.

Makes: 6 Servings

Cooking + Prep Time: 1 hour & 25 minutes

Ingredients:

- 1 lb. of cubed eggplant
- 1 cup of chick peas, white
- 8 & 3/4 oz. of cubed tomatoes
- 2 sliced onions, medium
- 2 tbsp. of garlic and ginger paste
- 1 tbsp. of pepper powder, black
- 1 tsp. of salt, sea
- 1/2 tsp. of powdered cinnamon
- 1/2 cup of oil, olive

Instructions:

1. Sauté eggplant in 1 tbsp. of oil on med-high in large skillet for 10-12 minutes, till crisp-tender and lightly browned.

2. Remove the eggplant from the pan. Set it aside.

3. In the same skillet on med-high, sauté the onions in the rest of the oil for six to eight minutes, till tender and light brown.

4. Add and stir ground pepper, cinnamon, sea salt, garlic and ginger. Cook for two to three minutes.

5. Add chick peas, eggplant and tomatoes and bring to a boil.

6. Reduce the heat to low and cover pan. Simmer for 1/2 hour till eggplant becomes tender.

7. Uncover pan. Cook for 12-15 minutes till most liquid has been absorbed. Serve hot.

Arabian Chicken Mugalgal

Mugalgal is a famous dish in the Middle East, especially in Saudi Arabia. It is a traditional dish that is served commonly during Eid al-Adha.

Makes: 4-6 Servings

Cooking + Prep Time: 1 hour & 10 minutes

Ingredients:

- 1 chicken, large, cut into pieces
- 1 tsp. of oil, vegetable
- 1 chopped onion, medium
- 1 tbsp. of spices, mixed
- 2 tbsp. of tomato paste
- 1 chopped tomato, medium
- 2 cups of water, filtered
- 1 strip-cut bell pepper, green, large
- 4 tbsp. of chopped coriander leaf
- 2 bouillon cubes, chicken
- 3 g. of black seed sesame

Instructions:

1. In deep fry pan, sear the pieces of chicken in oil till a bit golden. Add the onions. Continue to cook till soft.

2. Add spice mix and tomato paste. Sauté for one to two minutes, then add tomatoes. Cook for two more minutes.

3. Add water and bouillon cubes. Bring to boil. Stir ingredients till they are combined. Add the bell peppers. Simmer for 20-25 minutes.

4. Add and stir coriander leaves. Serve with steamed rice or flatbread.

Pickled Beets – Torshi

Torshi is a type of pickle that is created from beets or young turnips. There are many health benefits to beets, and you will enjoy the dish, as well – it's quite tasty.

Makes: various # of Servings

Cooking + Prep Time: 10 minutes prep + 7 days pickling time

Ingredients:

- 5 or 6 small-medium beets, raw
- 2-3 tbsp. of salt, kosher
- 6 cups of water, filtered
- 1 fresh lemon, juice only

Instructions:

1. Leave beets unpeeled and wash.

2. Cut in 1/4-inch slices.

3. Add kosher salt to filtered water. Mix well till salt has dissolved.

4. Drizzle the lemon juice on beets.

5. Spoon or pour beets into sterilized jars with lids.

6. Pour salted water sufficient to top beets into jars.

7. Seal jars. Place them in cool location for seven days or more. Open and serve.

Arabian Kabsa

Kabsa has been served in the Arab region for many years and is often made with chicken and rice. You can add nuts and vegetables, too. There are many different variations to the dish.

Makes:4-6 Servings

Cooking + Prep Time: 2 hours & 5 minutes

Ingredients:

- 5 cups of water, filtered
- 2 & 1/4 lbs. of cubed beef or lamb
- 3 tbsp. of oil, vegetable
- 2 sliced onions, medium
- 2 peeled, chopped tomatoes, medium
- 1 chili pepper, green
- 2 tsp. of cumin, ground
- 4 cardamom pods, whole
- 3/4 tsp. of pepper, black, ground
- 1 stick of cinnamon
- 1 tbsp. of tomato paste
- 2 bouillon cubes, chicken
- 2 & 1/2 cups of rice, basmati

Instructions:

1. Pour water and place meat cubes in large sized pot. Bring to a boil. Skim any froth that appears. Cover pot. Simmer on low heat for about an hour, till meat has become tender.

2. Heat oil in medium pot. Cook onions on med. heat for five to six minutes.

3. Add bouillon, tomato paste, cinnamon stick, ground pepper, powdered cardamom, cumin, chili pepper and tomatoes. Stir constantly while cooking for three to four minutes.

4. Add cooked meat and stock to pot. You should have about three cups of stock. Add more water if you need it.

5. Cover with rice. Bring to a boil. Cover and cook on low heat for 18-20 minutes, till rice has cooked.

6. Pour into large sized serving dish. Garnish using some pine seeds, almonds and raisins, if desired. Serve.

Chicken Haleem

Muslims enjoy Haleem very much, because of its spicy, creamy taste. It is rich in nutrition, as well, and will probably be quite popular with your family and guests.

Makes:6-8 Servings

Cooking + Prep Time: 55 minutes

Ingredients:

- 1 lb. of boneless chicken
- 1 cup of boiled wheat
- 1 cup of boiled lentils
- 2 tsp. of chili powder, red
- 1 tsp. of salt, sea
- 1/2 tsp. of turmeric
- 1/2 tsp. of powdered mace and nutmeg
- 1 tsp. of powdered allspice
- 1 tsp. of crushed cumin
- 2 tsp. of garlic ginger paste
- 2 fried onions
- 1 unfried onion
- 1/2 cup of oil, olive

To garnish:

- Coriander, fresh
- Lemon, fresh
- Mint leaves, chopped
- Chopped green chilies
- Ginger
- Chaat Masala spice powder

Instructions:

1. Cook chicken in large pan on low heat with 1 glass water, salt, cumin, turmeric, red chili powder and garlic ginger paste.

2. Shred chicken when it becomes tender.

3. Blend the wheat and lentils.

4. Add chicken mixture with 1 cup water and the fried onions.

5. Cook for 1/2 hour while continuously mashing.

6. Add mace and nutmeg powder and allspice.

7. Heat the oil. Add raw onions. Fry till it is a golden-brown color.

8. Pour mixture on Haleem. Use your choice of ingredients to garnish. Serve hot.

Rice Boukhari

Boukhari rice, what a flavorful and aromatic rice dish! It features a number of spices that are meant to help in evoking the memory of the place from whence its name comes – the city of Boukhari.

Makes: 5-6 Servings

Cooking + Prep Time: 2 hours & 35 minutes

Ingredients:

- 3 tbsp. of butter, clarified
- 1 & 1/2 lb. of lamb, bone-in, sliced in pieces
- 3 chopped onions, medium
- 8 cups of water, filtered
- 2 bouillon cubes, mutton
- 2 bouillon cubes, chicken
- 3/4 tsp. each of ground cardamom, cumin and pepper, black
- 3 pureed tomatoes, medium
- 2 & 1/2 cups of washed, drained rice
- 2 thin-sliced, boiled carrots
- 1 cup of mixed nuts, fried

Instructions:

1. Heat the clarified butter in large sized pot. Brown pieces of lamb till they are a golden-brown color. Add the onions. Stir now and then till they are golden-brown, as well.

2. Add the water, chicken bouillon, tomato juice and all spices. Cover. Cook on low heat for an hour and a half, till meat has cooked fully.

3. After meat has cooked, add rice to meat stock. You should have about four cups of stock. Cover. Cook on low for 20-25 minutes till rice has cooked fully.

4. Place rice on large sized serving dish. Put meat on top. Add cooked carrots atop meat. Garnish and serve.

Grilled Arab Kebabs

Kebabs are hearty, and popular in the Arab world for many occasions. They are especially welcome during the summer months, when outdoor cooking is at its best.

Makes:5-7 Servings

Cooking + Prep Time: 35 minutes

Ingredients:

- 2 & 1/4 lb. of mince, beef or mutton
- 1 tsp. of chili powder, red
- 1/2 tsp. of chili, pounded
- 1/2 tsp. of allspice powder
- 1/2 tsp. of kebab cheni spice
- 2 slices of bread
- 1 tbsp. of roasted, powdered cumin seed
- 8 to 10 chilies, green
- 2 tbsp. of garlic ginger paste
- 1 small onion
- 2 tbsp. of skinned raw papaya paste
- 1 lemon, fresh
- Salt, sea, as desired
- Oil, olive, as needed

Instructions:

1. Mix all the ingredients and chop in food processor.

2. Marinate mixture for an hour in the refrigerator.

3. Prepare flat, oval shaped kebabs. Grill one at a time.

4. Use brush to apply oil. Turn meat till it is well tenderized.
Serve.

Meat and Okra Stew

This is a hearty stew that is brimming with flavor. Plus, it doesn't include unhealthy ingredients, such as gluten or sugar. It is satisfying, filling and nutritious.

Makes: 5-6 Servings

Cooking + Prep Time: 2 & 1/2 hours

Ingredients:

- 5 cups of water, filtered
- 1 lb. of cubed lamb
- 1/2 tsp. of spice mixture
- 2 mutton bouillon cubes
- 2 tbsp. of oil, vegetable
- 2 chopped onions, medium
- 6 chopped tomatoes, medium
- 1 lb. of frozen then thawed small okra
- 6 crushed garlic cloves
- 1 chili pepper, green, small

Instructions:

1. Add the water and cubed lamb meat to a large sized sauce pan. Bring to a boil. Skim any froth that appears on top.

2. Season lamb in pan with spices. Add bouillon cubes. Simmer on low for an hour, till meat becomes tender. Remove pieces of meat from stock. Set them aside.

3. Heat the oil in large sized pan and use it to cook one tomato and onions for three to four minutes. Add the okra. Stir for four to five minutes.

4. Use food processor to blend the rest of the tomato with lamb stock. Add this mixture to okra pan. Cover. Simmer for 12-15 minutes, till the okra has cooked.

5. Fry green chili and garlic for a minute. Add to okra stew, along with lamb pieces. Allow to simmer for three to five minutes. Serve hot.

Sheer Khurma

Prepared with nuts and milk, this tasteful vermicelli recipe is a nutritious dish for everyday meals or special occasions.

Makes:3-5 Servings

Cooking + Prep Time: 50 minutes

Ingredients:

- 7 oz. of vermicelli
- 67 & 1/2 fluid ounces of milk, whole
- 8 & 3/4 oz. of sugar, granulated
- 1/4 tsp. of saffron coloring
- 3 & 1/2 oz. of butter, clarified
- 10 sliced almonds
- 10 sliced pistachios
- 1/3 oz. of raisins
- 3 & 1/2 oz. of sliced dates
- 3 cardamoms, green
- 2 sticks of cinnamon
- 3 cloves

Instructions:

1. Heat the butter in medium pan. Add vermicelli, raisins, pistachios, almonds, dates, cardamoms, cloves and sticks of cinnamon.

2. Continuously stir. Add milk. Cook over med. heat.

3. Add saffron coloring and sugar. Cook till mixture starts boiling. Serve warm or chill and serve cold.

Arabian Meat Kebab – Kebab el Mirou

When Kebab el Mirou is made in an authentic way, as it is in this recipe, it is wholesome and filling. It will inspire you to try your hand at other Arabian recipes, too.

Makes: 4-6 Servings

Cooking + Prep Time: 35 minutes

Ingredients:

- 1 lb. of beef, minced
- 1/2 cup of flour, all-purpose
- 3/4 tsp. of pepper, black, ground
- 1/2 tsp. of cinnamon, ground
- 1 tsp. of coriander, ground
- 3 crushed garlic cloves
- 1 egg, large
- 2 chicken bouillon cubes, dissolved in 1/4 cup of filtered water
- 2 tbsp. of oil, vegetable

Instructions:

1. Mix meat in large sized bowl with dissolved bouillon, egg, garlic, all the spices and flour, till the mixture is combined well. Divide it into small balls of the same approximate size.

2. Heat the oil in large sized fry pan. Fry meatballs for four to five minutes, till they are lightly browned. Serve hot.

Ash Reshteh Soup

Ash reshteh soup is originally a Persian dish, carried over to Arabian kitchens. It includes lentils, chick peas and beans, along with noodles and healthy green herbs.

Makes:4-6 Servings

Cooking + Prep Time: 55 minutes

Ingredients:

- 1 cup cooked, each of brown lentils, chick peas and kidney beans
- 2 chopped onions, medium + extra for garnishing
- 3 crushed garlic cloves
- 1 cup of dry noodles, gluten-free if available
- 1 small bunch chopped cilantro
- Chopped spring onions, parsley and dill
- 1 cup spinach, baby
- Optional: 1/2 bouillon cube
- 1 tbsp. of curry power
- 2 tbsp. of oil, coconut
- 1 tsp. of turmeric powder
- 2 & 1/2 cups of water

Instructions:

1. Sauté 1/2 the onions and 1 tbsp. coconut oil in large sized pot. Add garlic. Cook for about four minutes over med. heat, till onions become translucent.

2. Add 1/2 of your water, plus lentils and beans. Allow to boil for several minutes. Add spinach and chopped herbs.

3. Add stock cube and seasonings. Allow to simmer for 8-10 minutes, till flavor has intensified and the greens have cooked down.

4. Break noodles and add to pot. Add remainder of water. Simmer till the noodles have cooked. Season as desired.

5. Lightly fry the rest of the onions till they become golden. Garnish. Serve.

Arabian Tomato and Lamb

This lamb recipe made with tomatoes is beautifully prepared, and a delight for you to enjoy sharing with your family or with dinner guests. You can serve it with harissa sauce, if you like, and with naan flat bread on the side.

Makes:3-4 Servings

Cooking + Prep Time: 1 hour & 55 minutes

Ingredients:

- 2 tbsp. of butter, clarified
- 3 sticks of cinnamon, small
- 4 cloves, whole
- 2 & 1/4 lbs. pieces of lamb, bone-in
- 3 pureed tomatoes, medium
- 1 tbsp. of tomato paste
- 3/4 tsp. of pepper, black, ground
- 1 tsp. of cumin, ground
- 2 chicken bouillon cubes
- 3 cups of water, filtered

Instructions:

1. Heat clarified butter in large sized pot. Add cloves and sticks of cinnamon. Stir swiftly for 8-10 seconds, then add lamb. Stir for two to three minutes.

2. Add the bouillon, cumin, ground pepper, tomato paste, water and tomato puree.

3. Bring mixture to a boil, then cover and allow to simmer on low heat for an hour and a half. Meat should be tender, and the mixture should still include some sauce.

4. Place meat on serving dish. Add sauce. Serve.

Leg of Mutton Roast – Raan Roast

Mutton roast leg, also known as raan roast, can be the center of a wonderful meal, when presented decoratively. It goes well with many side dishes, too.

Makes:4-6 Servings

Cooking + Prep Time: 1 & 1/2 hour

Ingredients:

- 1 leg of mutton (raan)
- 8 & 3/4 oz. of yogurt, low-fat
- 1/2 cup of milk, 2%
- 1/2 tsp. of saffron
- 4 tbsp. of oil, olive
- 1 tsp. of Garam Masala spice mix
- Sea salt, as desired
- 1 x 2" pc. of chopped ginger
- 6 chopped cloves of garlic
- 1 tbsp. of chili flakes, crushed
- 1 tsp. of ground cumin seed, roasted
- 1 whole onion, medium
- 5 or 6 chilies, green
- 2 spring onions

Instructions:

1. Warm 1/2 cup of milk in a pan. Add saffron and stir it well.

2. Use a knife to make cut marks on both sides of leg of lamb. Rub in Garam masala on each side. Allow to set for 10-12 minutes.

3. Add the yogurt, cumin, chili flakes, oil, garlic, ginger, salt, yogurt and diluted saffron made in step 1 to a bowl. Combine well.

4. Pour solution from step 3 over mutton. Rub well. Allow to sit for 15-18 additional minutes.

5. Place mutton on baking tray. Put chilies, onion and spring onion over the top. Place in 350F oven for 10-12 minutes. Turn the mutton over. Allow it to bake for 10-12 more minutes.

6. Remove leg of mutton from pan and pour the juices to a separate pan. Place leg of lamb on large serving plate.

7. To prepare garnish, blend the spring onion, regular onion and green chilies in food processor. Add back to juices from mutton pan. Bake till it becomes saucy, with a thick consistency. Pour over leg of mutton and serve.

Arabian Almento Patties

Almento patties are made by steaming the tasty dough. This recipe is an authentic one, served as an Iftar feast.

Makes:8 Servings

Cooking + Prep Time: 1 hour & 40 minutes

Ingredients:

- 3 cups of flour, plain
- 1 tsp. of salt, sea
- 1 egg, large
- 1 cup of water, filtered
- For stuffing
- 1 & 2/3 lbs. of lamb, minced
- 2 chopped onions, medium
- 1 tsp. of pepper, black, ground
- 3 tbsp. of water, filtered, mixed with 2 chicken bouillon cubes

Instructions:

1. Combine the egg, flour and salt in large sized bowl. Add water gradually, mixing ingredients till they have formed a well-mixed dough. You can add additional water if you need to.

2. Divide dough into equal sized, small portions. Form them into balls. Cover them and set them aside. Allow to rest for about an hour.

3. Combine mince with dissolved bouillon cubes, onions and ground pepper. Set it aside.

4. Roll out balls. Stuff them with 1 tsp. meat mixture. Fold and enclose them.

5. Grease large steamer-pot with clarified butter. Place dough patties in steamer basket.

6. Fill 1/2 of steamer pot bottom section with heated water. Add a bit of salt. Cover. Seal pot well. Place pot on med. heat for 45-50 minutes till patties have cooked fully.

7. Arrange patties on dishes. Serve them hot.

Spiced Chicken Shawarma

You can make Shawarma at home when you use this chef-inspired recipe. There are no hard-to-find ingredients needed to prepare it for your family and friends.

Makes: various # of servings

Cooking + Prep Time: 50 minutes

Ingredients:

- 1 lb. of boneless chicken
- 3 or 4 cloves of garlic
- 1/2 cup of yogurt
- 2 tbsp. of vinegar
- 2 tbsp. of chili paste, red
- 1 tbsp. of lemon juice, fresh
- 2 to 3 tbsp. of oil, olive
- Salt, sea, as desired
- Tahini sauce, as desired

For the salad:

- 1 cup of pickled chili
- 1/2 cup of pickled cucumber
- 1 cucumber
- 1 onion
- 1 tomato, ripe
- 3 or 4 chopped leaves of lettuce
- 1/2 cup of green or black olives, as preferred
- 2 to 3 tbsp. of oil, olive

As desired: pita bread

Instructions:

1. Cut the chicken into slices, thinly.

2. Add oil, garlic and sliced chicken to pan. Stir fry them. Add chili paste, salt, lemon juice and yogurt. Mix well. Stir fry. When water has dried, remove to plate.

3. Place salad ingredients in large sized bowl and gently toss them.

4. To assemble: toast pita breads lightly. Cut them into pockets. Fill with salad, sauce and chicken. Serve while still warm.

Noodle & Shish Barak Soup

This dish originated in Lebanon, possibly from origins in the Turk and Ottoman empires. It is made with tasty noodles cooked in a plain stew. It is a traditional dish, much like other home stews cooked in the Arab region.

Makes:5 Servings

Cooking + Prep Time: 25 minutes

Ingredients:

- 6 cups of water, filtered
- 2 tsp. of tomato paste
- 1 sachet of soup, spring seasoning
- 7 oz. of shish barak, prepared
- 2 tbsp. of chopped coriander leaves

Instructions:

1. Add tomato paste, soup sachet and water to large sized sauce pan.

2. Bring to a boil. Simmer on low for five minutes. Add shish barak. Simmer for five more minutes, till shish barak have cooked.

3. Use coriander for garnishing. Serve.

Tahinah Salad

This is an easy-to-make salad that offers a bundle of healthy vegetables. The Tahinah sauce gives it even more flavor, and you can serve it any time.

Makes:4 Servings

Cooking + Prep Time: 25 minutes

Ingredients:

- 5 & 1/3 oz. of carrots
- 7 oz. of potatoes
- 3 & 1/2 oz. of beans
- 3 & 1/2 oz. of peas
- 7 oz. of cubed tomatoes
- 3 & 1/2 oz. of chopped parsley
- 3 & 1/2 oz. of Tahinah sauce
- 2 tbsp. of lemon juice, fresh if available
- Sea salt & ground pepper, as desired

Instructions:

1. Peel the potato and carrot and cut them into cubes.

2. Boil the peas, beans, carrots and potatoes till all are soft. Then drain water. Allow veggies to cool.

3. Mix a bit of water with tahinah sauce and lemon juice.

4. Add boiled vegetables, along with tahinah sauce, parsley and tomatoes to bowl. Season as desired. Toss gently and chill in refrigerator before serving.

Arabian Rice with Potato and Lamb

This tasty dish is usually made with lamb, but can also be created with ground turkey, if lamb meat is not easy to find in your area. It is especially tasty when you serve it with Naan bread.

Makes:4-5 Servings

Cooking + Prep Time: 1 hour & 10 minutes

Ingredients:

- 2 cups of oil, vegetable, to fry
- 2 cubed potatoes, medium
- 1 chopped onion, medium
- 2 crushed garlic cloves
- 8 & 3/4 oz. of lamb, minced
- 2 halved limes, dried
- 1/4 tsp. ground each of cumin, cinnamon, cardamom and pepper, black
- 2 chicken bouillon cubes
- 1/4 tsp. of filaments, saffron
- 1 tbsp. of tomato paste
- 4 & 1/2 cups of water, filtered
- 2 & 1/2 cups of washed, drained rice, basmati

Instructions:

1. Heat the oil in saucepan, while reserving 3 tbsp. Fry cubed potatoes till they are tender and a golden color. Set them aside.

2. Heat remaining 3 tbsp. of oil in large sized pot. Fry the onions for three to four minutes, till they are golden in color. Add garlic. Stir for a minute more.

3. Add lamb. Fry for four to five minutes, till it browns. Add tomato paste, bouillon cubes, spices and dried limes. Stir for a minute. Add water. Bring to a boil.

4. Add fried potatoes and rice. Bring to boil while stirring occasionally. Cover pot. Simmer over low heat for 20 to 25 minutes, till rice has cooked. Serve hot.

Olive Fried Rice

You can spice up a simple recipe with olives' delicate flavors. This dish is usually topped with roasted capsicum, and it's an eye-appealing, as well as delicious, Arabian dish.

Makes:4 Servings

Cooking + Prep Time: 40 minutes

Ingredients:

- 10 & 1/2 oz. of Sela rice, boiled
- 1 tbsp. of garlic, chopped finely
- 1 onion chopped
- 2 tomatoes, ripe
- 1/2 tsp. of pepper, black, crushed
- 1 tsp. of paprika
- 1 cup of olives
- 1 cubed carrot
- 2 Capsicum pods
- 1 tbsp. of lemon juice, fresh if available
- 1 to 2 tsp. of oil, olive
- Salt, sea, as desired

Instructions:

1. Grease the capsicum with one or two tsp. oil. Roast in oven. Slice into rings. Set them aside.

2. Add oil to pan. Sauté onion and garlic. Add tomatoes and fry them.

3. Add paprika, crushed pepper, olives and carrot. Season as desired and then stir fry.

4. Add the boiled rice. Cook till flavors have combined.

5. Add roasted capsicum and lemon juice. Combine well. Place on platter. Serve.

Arabian Dessert Recipes

Pistachio Cake

This tasty cake can be served with milk glaze and confectioner's sugar or by simply dusting it with confectioner's sugar alone. Adding cardamom

Makes:the cake more aromatic.

Makes:10 Servings

Cooking + Prep Time: 1 hour & 15 minutes

Ingredients:

For cake:

- 1 & 1/2 cups of sugar, granulated
- 1 cup of yogurt, Greek
- 1 tbsp. of vanilla, pure
- 1 & 1/2 cups of flour, all-purpose
- 1 & 1/2 cups of pistachios, ground
- 1 tsp. baking soda
- 4 eggs, large
- 1 & 1/2 tsp. baking powder
- 2 sticks of room temperature butter, unsalted
- 1 tsp. of salt, sea

For glazing:

- 1/2 cup of sugar, confectioner's
- 2 tbsp. of milk, whole
- 1/4 tsp. of cardamom, ground
- A dash of sea salt

Instructions:

1. Preheat oven to 350F. Butter & flour Bundt pan.

2. Beat sugar and eggs together with mixer, till color lightens. Add yogurt, butter and vanilla and beat them into the mixture.

3. Pour pistachio nuts into food processor. Pulse till they are ground.

4. In separate bowl, sift salt, baking soda, baking powder, ground pistachios and flour together. Beat dry ingredients into wet ingredients.

5. Pour batter into Bundt pan. Bake at 350F for 45-50 minutes. Inserted toothpick should come back clean. Set aside to cool.

6. To prepare glaze, whisk salt, cardamom, milk and confectioner's sugar till you have a smooth mixture. Drizzle over cake after it cools. Sprinkle on extra pistachios, as desired. Serve.

Sweet Arab Dough Balls

What a tasty treat for any day or evening! It features small dough balls fried to a crispy, golden brown and coated with syrup. Make plenty, because they disappear very quickly!

Makes:6-8 Servings

Cooking + Prep Time: 1/2 hour

Ingredients:

- 1 tsp. of yeast
- 1 pinch sugar, granulated
- 2 cups of flour, plain
- 2 tbsp. of flour, corn
- 3 tbsp. of powdered milk, full cream
- 1 pinch sea salt
- 1 & 1/2 cups of water, filtered
- 2 cups of oil to fry
- 2 cups of syrup, sugar

Instructions:

1. Combine 1/2 cup of filtered water with yeast and pinch of granulated sugar in small sized bowl.

2. In separate bowl, combine pinch of salt, powdered milk, flour and corn flour. Add yeast mixture. Rub ingredients using your fingertips till they look like bread crumbs.

3. Add water a bit at a time. Mix well to form a soft dough. Cover. Set aside for an hour and a half, till dough size doubles.

4. Divide dough into balls, about the size of whole walnuts. Deep fry balls in 350F oil for six to eight minutes, till they are golden brown in color.

5. Dip fried dough balls in sugar syrup for a couple minutes. Remove them and serve.

Arab Caramel Cardamom Pears

Caramel apples are quite famous in many parts of the world, but caramel pears are a treat that must be tried to be believed. They can be presented in a pretty way at special dinners, too.

Makes: 4 Servings

Cooking + Prep Time: 40 minutes

Ingredients:

- 1 cup of sugar, granulated
- 1 & 1/4 cups of cream, heavy, warmed a bit
- 1 tbsp. of butter, unsalted
- 1/2 tsp. of cardamom, ground
- Salt, sea, as desired
- 4 washed, cored pears

Instructions:

1. Add 1 cup sugar to heavy-bottomed pot. Heat over low till it has melted and begins lightly browning. Don't stir it much or it will become lumpy. Keep an eye on it, so it doesn't burn.

2. Once sugar is lightly golden brown and bubbling, add cream. Be ready for the mixture to bubble. Stir till cream has incorporated fully. Add butter and stir.

3. If mixture has some hard lumps, continue to stir over low heat till they finish melting. Then your sauce will be smooth.

4. Add cardamom and stir. Season as desired.

5. Wash, then dry pears. Remove core and seeds. Hold pears by stems and dip them into warmed caramel sauce till coated fully. Place on rack so they don't drip on anything. Allow them to sit until caramel hardens and then serve.

Arabian Sweet Cheese Bake

All through the Arab region, sweet cheese is a popular dessert. It's a rich and delicious treat, using cheese baked in tasty dough and soaked in syrup.

Makes: 5-7 Servings

Cooking + Prep Time: 1 hour & 10 minutes

Ingredients:

- 1 & 1/2 cups of grated, unsalted cheese, white baladi
- 3/4 cup of melted butter, unsalted
- 1 egg, large
- 1/2 cup of milk powder, full cream
- 1 tin of Nestlé® Original Cream
- 1 pinch salt, sea
- 1 pinch sugar, granulated
- 1 cup of flour, plain
- 1/2 tbsp. of baking powder
- 1 cup of syrup, sugar

Instructions:

1. Combine egg mixture, grated cheese and batter well in large sized bowl.

2. Add Nestle® Cream, powdered milk, sugar and salt. Combine.

3. Mix baking powder with flour. Sift over it and combine.

4. Spread mixture in round pan. Bake at 325F for 30-40 minutes, till it's done.

5. Remove from the oven. Pour syrup over cheese evenly. Serve.

Arabian Bread Pudding

This is an Arabian version of Asian Shahi Tukray and English bread pudding. Use plenty of raisins and coconut, since they are the heart of the recipe.

Makes:2-4 Servings

Cooking + Prep Time: 45 minutes

Ingredients:

- 5 & 1/3 oz. of spiced flat bread - Baqarkhani
- 2 cups of milk, whole
- 4 tbsp. of sugar, granulated
- 2 oz. of crushed almonds
- 2 oz. of crushed walnuts
- 2 oz. of raisins
- 1 oz. of coconut, desiccated
- 1 cup of whipped cream

Instructions:

1. Heat the milk up. Add the sugar.

2. Cook in pan till the sugar has dissolved. Remove.

3. Break flat breads. Spread in glass baking dish.

4. Use walnuts, almonds, raisins & coconut in layers.

5. Pour milk gently over mixture.

6. Spread the cream on the top.

7. Bake at 350F for 20-25 minutes. Remove and serve warm.

Conclusion

This Arabian cookbook has shown you…

…How to use different ingredients to affect unique Arabic tastes in dishes both well-known and rare. How can you include it in your own Arab recipes?

You can…

Make Arabian breakfast dishes, which not many people know about. They are just as tasty as breakfast dishes found in other areas of the world.

Learn to cook with sumac spice, mastic resin, mahlab aromatic spice and zaatar. You can find these in many Middle Eastern groceries.

Enjoy making delectable lamb and beef recipes favored in the Arabian Peninsula. They have tasty ways of preparing meat and fish as well, and there are SO many ways to make these recipes taste authentic.

Make dishes using cardamom and freekeh, or roasted wheat, which are often used in Arabian cooking.

Make various types of pastries like cheese bake desserts and cardamom pears, which will tempt your family's sweet tooth.

Have fun experimenting! Enjoy the results!

Dear Reader,

Thank you very much for choosing my book. I hope you really enjoy it. If don't mind I would like to ask you to leave a review after reading.

Thanks.

Sincerely yours,

Stephanie Sharp

For announcements about new releases, please follow my author page on Amazon.com! (Look for the Follow Bottom under the photo) You can find that at *https://www.amazon.com/author/stephanie-sharp* or Scan QR-code below.